30.10.12
With Love,
Brigitte xx

Teenage
Relationships

The Breakthrough Guide to Untangling your Heart Strings

I love you, so glad i met you!
-Chloe (random hug girl)
xx

Brigitte Sumner

with Jez and Lionel Sumner and Friends

MyVoice

My Voice Publishing
Unit 1 16 Maple Road
EASTBOURNE
BN23 6NY
www.myvoicepublishing.com

Published by MVP July 2011

© Brigitte Sumner 2011

Brigitte Sumner asserts the moral right to be identified as the author of this work.

Cover design: Myles Hersee www.lightningguy.deviantart.com
Design: My Voice Publishing

ISBN 978-0-9569682-1-0

Introduction

Welcome to This Book.

We wanted to put together a simple and concise guide for teenagers that offer a place where you can come with your questions. During your teenage years there are so many changes and at times that feels exciting. At other times it makes you feel a little scared or insecure.

We want you to know that you are not alone. You are not the only one going through these changes. You are not the only one who has these questions. There are a lot of answers to be found on the internet or from other resources. This book is different in that it tells you stories of real live teenagers who have experienced just what you are going through now.

This book is different because we have included tips and ideas from other young people who are either still teenagers or have freshly graduated from teenage-hood. They know and remember the questions they had. Growing up, they figured out answers. They share these with you here. These are by no means the only answers. Maybe they are even the wrong answers for you right now. And maybe they put you on the right track to find the answers that are right for you.

And then we have stories by older people, who, just like you, have been teenagers. Your parents, aunts, uncles and even your grandparents have been teenagers at some stage in their lives. There are some themes that seem to go with being a teenager, regardless of the era. And then there are issues that have to do with specific times. There is much more choice right now than there was fifty years ago. And when you read this book fifty years from the publishing date, there may be much more choice again.

I was born in the decade after the Second World War. My

parents were teenagers during that war. They were in their twenties when I was born as the eldest child in the family. I have two younger brothers. Most of Europe was fast rebuilding its wealth and getting to grips with post war life.

At school, milk was regularly provided to ensure that growing children had enough calcium to make strong bones.* As a result my generation grew taller faster as there is a lot of growth hormone in cow's milk (to ensure that small calves grow into big cows fast).

The world of fashion was still based on the outdated sizes of pre-war women and men who were much shorter because they consumed less dairy products. Production of clothing had not caught up with the new sizes and shapes of children. All garments were too short and too wide for a lot of us. If the length fit, it was miles too wide. If the width fit, it was way too short.

As a teenager, I grew much earlier and faster than my peers, so I stood out in that sense. I also stood out because I am half Chinese and most of my peers were blond and blue eyed.

So picture tall, half Chinese, braces (so no smiles with teeth), jam jar glasses (move over Ugly Betty...). I was very self conscious. Very shy. And very insecure entering my teenage years.

It felt awkward being the tallest girl in class and it was a relief when other girls caught up during the first two years in secondary school. Most of the boys took a few years longer.

During my teenage years I had many experiences. I searched for my own identity. I learned how to relate to boys. I had my first exclusive relationships. I found that my relationships with girls changed. I adjusted to the different ways to relate

* research has since proven that milk actually leaches the bones of calcium

to my parents. I explored how to look after my body in a healthy way. I found it hard to cope with bullying behaviour by others at school. And even harder when I was the bully myself. Those were some of the challenges I experienced as a teenager.

I excelled during some of the time of my teenage years. I became confident, discovered talents in art, music and strengths in sports. I learned to relate to the world around me. I found that my tall body could run, ski and swim fast.

I discovered the power and strength of my body. I found how to relate to boys and how to be intimate. I learned to embrace my gifts and talents. I enjoyed being with other girls and how to be positive about each other and to give each other support. Those were some of the delights I experienced as a teenager.

My teenage years were sprinkled with different emotions.

When both my sons went through similar experiences, many of my own memories of that age floated back to the surface of my mind. I watched them and their friends learn and grow through this time. I realised that there was no book that provides support for the challenges of that stage in life. That is how the idea of this guide came about.

We are delighted to bring you the first edition of this book. We want to ask you a favour. As you go through the book and through your own teenage years, please let us know your tips, your experiences and your ideas. And make sure to take advantage of our exclusive offer at the back of the book, so you can speak personally to me or one of our trained coaches.

We want to know what YOU do to create healthy relationships and untangle heart strings.

That way, we can keep updating content for the follow up

books, the website and the iphone app.

Brigitte, Jez and Lionel Sumner.

July 2011.

Acknowledgements

This book started as a desperate search on the internet to find resources where my – then - teenage sons, Jeremy (Jez) and Lionel, could find information about more than just the biological facts that dominate the teenage years.

The information was either absent, hard to find or embedded within topics that did not relate to their questions.

Over the years since our household hit the teenage years, about a decade ago, until now, I have collated their questions, their solutions and their stories.

Many of Jez and lionel's friends have shared their experiences and stories too. They talked very openly about things close to their heart. I am grateful for and humbled by their openness, their honesty, their wisdom and their clarity.

Our thanks goes to the following people, who have contributed in some way, they are not mentioned in order of importance and if your name is not mentioned, please know that you have helped and contributed in some way to bring this guide into being.

Matt, Danny, Angela, Eric, Becky, Jack, Jessica, Sophie, Sandra, Enrique, Sam, Kitty, Pat, Jo, James, Alex, Maria, Dipti, Brian, Menno, Marie, Samadarshini, Gordon, Yvonne, Amanda Jane, Ben, Tony, Kari, Emma, Sofie, Felicity, Kim, Pam, Deb, Mims, Peter, Robbie, Patrick, Steve, Andrew, John, Nigel, Chris, Mairin, Anna, Antonio, Juliet, Jenn, Caroline, Sage, Geeta, Vicki, Marlon, Brenda, Joe, Fernando, Hugo, Linda, Tina, Elly, Zac, Krishnaraj, Allan, Marc, Ellen, Robert, Paula, Maarten, Loren, Maggie, Su, Hans, Nico, Karin, Toos, Joep, Tom, Pieter, Luuk, Irma, Paul, Gerry, Ans, Tim, Susie, George, Art, Sandy, Rachelle, Jette, Margot, Colin, Belinda, Marijke, Ed, Doris, Saskia, Julia, Marlies, Fiona, Monique, Sally, Cees, Stuart, Michelle, Bob, Ray, Sofia, Ad, Pam,

Buzz, Tammy, Stuart, Connie, Mike, Ashley, Onno, Harry, Felix, Ross and Phoebe.

And of course as ever for your loving and patient support to Rex, Dad, who manouvered the ship of our family through many calm and stormy teenage waters.

Dedication

To all the teenagers of the world. Life is about relationships. You are the leaders of the future. Having healthy relationships now, sets you up for having healthy relationships later. You are the role models of the future.

You are the guardians of this planet.

Special Offer!

Would you like to speak to the author, Brigitte Sumner*
Well known Relationship and Communication Coach?**

Simply go to our website www.teenagerelationship.info
and leave your email address for us to contact you and
give you a Free 10 min Phone Session where you can ask
any of your relationship questions!

*or one of our specially trained coaches

** Brigitte Sumner's books have appeared on the Amazon
bestselling Relationship Books List

Contents

Chapter One

Growing Up

Teenage years are so interesting. You can have so much fun. And yet, they can sometimes feel so painful. There is a lot of unknown territory to explore. A lot of growing to do. Physical growing and emotional growing and even spiritual growing.

The first relationship in life is with our parents. From literally being part of our parents, we become physically separate beings at birth. Still depending on our parents completely, we take more time to become independent than most mammals and other animals.

The first time we realise that we are separate from our parents and our environment is during the early toddler years. We discover the words 'I' and 'me'. We start with calling ourselves by our own name. We say 'Jenny's toy' and mean 'my toy'. When asked 'who is this?' when someone points at us, we say 'Jenny!' instead of 'me!' The words 'I' and 'me' arrive at a later stage in our psychological and language development. Before that, we really do not feel that separate from another. We cry in sympathy with another person, animal or even a plant as we really DO feel their pain. We mostly lose that ability but can develop it again later, when we want.

The sense of separation continues during our lives and manifests strongly during the teenage years. We feel separate. We feel different than someone else. We feel that we are the only one who feels the way we do. Yet, there is an even stronger sense and tendency to deny that we feel this way or that. We hope that no one will be able to find out that we are actually pretending and faking our feelings in order to mask our true feelings.

During our upbringing and schooling, we have learned that

certain behaviour is 'right' and that certain behaviour is 'wrong'. When we're a baby, our parents and care takers beam with delight when we burp, fart and fill our pants. Without warning, the rules of the game change. At around the age of two or three, burping, farting and filling our pants are not the done thing.

When we burp, we are encouraged to do this quietly or say 'excuse me,' farting is a more serious offence as even when done on the quiet, there is an added give away of smell. Someone with a great sense of smell will always detect the change in air quality and before you know it, ask 'now, who has let that one off?'

As for filling our pants, that becomes very unacceptable past the age of three and really should be done on a potty or toilet. If this still persists, parents tend to consult doctors, clever books and internet sites for solutions to this problem.

In some cultures, burping is a sign that you really enjoyed your food and farting just means that you have to let out wind. As far as I know, filling your pants beyond early childhood is not really a done thing in any culture.

We learn many unwritten rules throughout childhood. What is mine is mine and what is not mine, belongs to someone else. However much I want it, I have to ask if I can borrow it or keep it. I can't just take it. Growing up, we learn how to 'play nicely' and 'share', say 'please' and 'thank you' and if we forget any of those very difficult rules, we get reminded or reprimanded.

We get conditioned, just like other mammals and animals to behave the way our environment wants us to. Being a teenager provides us with time to discover our own freedom, our boundaries and restrictions and freedom of our body. We learn how to be independent of our parents and socialise more with our peers, we learn how to work more in teams, how and when to be a leader and how and when to comply with the rules of society. In some cultures there is still a clear divide between childhood and adulthood, where the young person must pass a number of initiations, tests and challenges in order to show how they can operate independently of their elders.

Because we have now entered the world of the adults, we behave like adults. We stop playing, we stop skipping and running just for the fun of it. We walk slowly. We laugh less. We become more serious. Teenage boys walk very slow, walking fast reminds them of their childhood. Therefore they have labelled it childish to walk fast, or skip or run for no reason. Even teenage primates drag their limbs the same way human teenagers do. The swagger seems to be universal across several species.

Peer pressure becomes much more important than what our parents think and say. Our parents fear that they loose control and in order to alley their own fears, very often impose strict rules that don't really work for teenagers any longer.

QUIZ

Let's see what you know about the development from baby to teenager?

Do this quiz to find out.

1. How does a baby communicate with his/her Mum or Dad?

    a. With words

    b. By crying, there are different ways of crying that all mean different things

    c. By mobile phone

2. What are some of the milestones in the life of a toddler?

    a. Riding a bicycle

    b. First tooth, first step, first word

    c. Cooking a meal

3. Who are the most likely people that you have your first relationships with?

    a. The neighbour

    b. Your Mum and Dad

    c. The football coach

4. What age is a child when they first start to talk?

    a. 1 month

    b. Around 1 year

    c. At 17 years old

5. What is the age when a child discovers the 'me' and 'not me'?

    a. 6

    b. Around 2 or 3

    c. 21

6. What is a big change in a child's life around the age of 5/6?

    a. It learns how to ski

b. It goes to school for the first time and learns to read and write

c. It gets a driving license

7. What hormone takes care of physical change in girls in puberty?

   a. Shemersheen

   b. Oestrogen

   c. Coffeebean

8. What hormone makes boys bodies change in puberty?

   a. Hemersheen

   b. Testosterone

   c. Tattoomachine

9. What 3 physical changes take place in girls during teenage years?

   a. Their knees start to shine, their fingers grow longer and they get curly toes

   b. Their breasts grow larger, they get their period and their hips grow wider

   c. Their hair grows, they stop playing football and they blush more

10. What 3 physical changes take place in boys during teenage years?

    a. Their arms get longer, their skin stretches and their

belly buttons change shape

b. Their penis gets larger, their voice gets lower and they grow taller

c. Their appetite for fruit increases, their saliva production increases and they grow hair between their toes

Mostly A: sorry, you have no clue, some of your answers may be nearly correct, but you better read a good biology book or look up online what really goes on.

Mostly B: Yes, you know exactly what happens.

Mostly C: again, no clue, read an informative book or ask a friend or friendly adult.

Now you are a teenager. Your relationships are changing. Some may need to be untangled. Read on.

Chapter Two

Your Relationship with Life

Tangled up with your relationship with Life?

- You find life so hard

- You find that life is not fair

- You don't believe that you have the life you want

- You don't have direction in life

The most important relationship in your life is the one with yourself. All other relationships are a mirror of the relationship you have with yourself. If many relationships in your life are tangled up, it is certain, that the relationship you have with yourself is tangled up.

How to create a good relationship with yourself

The three key ingredients to any relationship are trust, respect and communication. Do you trust yourself? Do you respect yourself? Do you communicate with yourself?

Building references

The quality of our lives depends on the quality of our questions.

We can always find evidence for something to be good.

And we can always find evidence for something to be bad.

When we constantly look for what is 'wrong' with ourselves, we will constantly find something that is 'wrong.' When we keep looking for what is 'great' about us, we will consistently find things that are 'great' about us.

Be your Own Best Friend

Do you have a best friend? Or at least a good friend? What do you say to your best friend? What do you say ABOUT your friend?

Now look what you say to yourself. Yes, the thoughts you think count as talking to yourself. Are they encouraging you? Or insulting you? Praising you? Or tearing you down?

Start by saying positive things to and about yourself.

Tips from Jez, Lionel and friends:

Who can you talk to and confide in that will listen? Find at least one person that can help you during this time.

Are you overwhelmed by the many areas of your life? Learn how to 'chunk' things down. Cut projects into bite size chunks that are actionable tasks and go through them one by one.

Life is not fair

Rather than looking at what is not working in your life, look beyond. Maybe you feel you have lost control over your life. You have control over how you feel. Do things that make you stronger and healthier so that you are able to cope better with the challenges of life.

Do you know what the life you want looks like? Create a treasure map. Cut out pictures of the life you DO want to live and write down inspiring words that encourage you. School years may seem endless but if you look at your life as a whole, they are only a small segment.

Your friends may know from an early age that they want to be a doctor or a professional football player. You have no idea. It worries you. Your parents say, do what you love and what makes you happy. One week this makes you happy, the next week that. Make a list of what you don't like, this eliminates a lot. The teenage years are years to find out. Most of your peers have no idea what they want to do with their lives. And honestly, not every adult knows either. Start to live fully rather than wait for a sign of what you should do with your life. Often, one thing leads to another. When you start, the next step shows up. But only when you start....

Exercise:

Write down three things that you like about you.

Write down three of your talents.

Write down three things that you are proud of.

Chapter Three

Your Relationship with your Body

Tangled up in your relationship with your Body:

- you feel awkward with your body

- You feel ugly

- You compare yourself with others

Your body has undergone massive changes. A bit like a building that has transformed from a bungalow or hut to a villa or even a block of flats and in some cases even a sky scraper! Some even have scaffolding to show for it (braces?). For some, this can take ages and for some it happens almost overnight. This can be a particular time that you feel a little or a lot of insecurity about your body. There is a lot of change and you are getting to grips with it physically, emotionally and energetically. Do you think that there is much more energy needed to fuel a sky scraper than a small one storey bungalow? You bet.

All this changing and growing can make you tired. You use up a lot of energy! Your whole system needs to rest more. According to Neil Stanley, a sleep researcher at the University of East Anglia and Jim Horne, director of Loughborough University's Sleep Research Centre young adults need more sleep than children or adults. Dr. Mary Carskadon, director of the Chronobiology and Sleep Research Laboratory at Bradley Hospital in East Providence, R.I. an adolescent sleep expert and co-chair of the foundation's sleep and teens task force, says pubescent changes in body chemistry make it difficult for teenagers to go to bed early and get up early.

Or maybe your body has NOT changed. You are fourteen and everyone in your class towers above you. You are adopted by others in school as their pet or a rare novelty. No one seems to notice that you are as mature and advanced as the guy who is nearly seven feet tall and has had a deep voice for the last eighteen months (the sky scraper from the previous paragraph). What is worse, no one takes you seriously. You may wonder whether you will stay small for the rest of your life? Your parents tell you that some grow early and some grow later. That is not much use at the moment.

Your body has started to grow. Your tried and trusted child body has grown hair in odd places and started to elongate and bulge in the most possible and impossible areas. Part of you wants to shout 'Give me my body back' and part of you is kind of curious what you will end up looking like. Believe me, the people we consider as the most beautiful on the planet still consider themselves ugly at times. I was amazed when I heard that Naomi Campbell (a supermodel who is paid millions of dollars just because she is beautiful) thinks that she is ugly at times. If even people like that feel ugly at times, then certainly it is a generic feeling that all of us have at times?

As a small child, you likely bumbled blissfully through the world of bodies without comparing yours to others. Growing up, we are trained and educated to spot differences (did you ever do one of those 'spot the difference' quizzes?). We then move on to see and point out differences between ourselves and others. During our teenage years we can become more self conscious, insecure and more aware of the difference between ourselves and others.

Because there is so much change going on during your teenage years you hardly get the opportunity to get used to one thing before the next thing comes up. Your pubic hair grows, you are just getting used to that and then you start to perspire profusely (and often smelly too!) and when you are just getting to grips with that, your voice drops an octave.

Or your breasts grow larger and you start to menstruate and you get mood swings. Nature just doesn't give you a lot of time to adjust to all these changes.

A story:

She sat on the doorstep. Her face was thunderclouding. Her heels were banging gently. Not too hard, they were bare. A frown. No words. Around her, the air was tangibly colder. No one understood. She was the only one. There was an impatience in her quirkiness. Her slender face, just lost the puppy fat her Mum said, which made her furious. Boys. They made her nervous. The ones she knew from before had vanished. Not really.

She just seemed to have become invisible to them. No wonder. Braces, glasses. Two years of smiling without teeth. If teeth showed, which they did by accident at times when she forgot, the reaction was devastating. As if some very ugly monster had been let out. People screamed. Ran. She inspected again the flags of spinach washed up between the metal groynes and miniscule elastic bands. Snogging. Not likely. Who'd want to snog her? And eat bits of decaying spinach in the process? A bit like seaweed hanging off the barnacles. No snogging. For at least another year. Her own tongue twirled around the scaffolding in her mouth. In the past her tongue had been impaled by some of the new wires. Imagine, some boys tongue stuck forever, just because he had snogged her a little too eagerly. The thought made her laugh.

Her chin rested on her knees, knobbly, the skin a little dry and grey. She sighed. Only two years ago, life was so much easier. She climbed. She ran. She fell on her knees all the time when trying to cross logs over ditches. Or jumped them. Her legs were the first to grow. Long. Endless. No trousers that fit. There was a lot of awkwardness now. Breasts. And periods. The started last summer. She banged her heels harder in thought. Last week. Emma and Georgie had inspected her face closely during the Physical Education lesson. Emma and Georgie had long hair. And they were very beautiful. They were best friends. They had nice clothes. And nice bags. Matching. They smiled nicely mostly. Mostly they did not look at her. But they did last week. Very closely. They looked at each other. And nodded. 'She has a moustache. Yes, she does'. They looked grave.

She swallowed. Had not noticed. At home she ran upstairs. Yes, they were right. There was a moustache. Very obviously. Now what? Her Mum said there wasn't one. Dad wasn't consulted. She could not go back to school. Not ever. Not with a moustache. She would stay home. Luckily, Mum understood. Conferred with her friend, Pam, the beautician. Mum went out at night and returned with a little bottle in her hand. With cotton buds the liquid was painted carefully on the slightly dark hairs. The hair was now blonde, and not very visible any longer.

Of course Emma and Georgie still saw it. From miles away even. But she learned that they talked. About other girls too. Her bum is so huge. She looks like an elephant. And her nose. You see the nose before you see her. And.....it went on and on

She licked her knee. It became more skin coloured. Last week Donald had looked at her. But he was talking to Harry at the same time. And they laughed, so maybe they laughed about her? She felt herself blush. And turned around in the corridor. Wanted to run. But felt silly. So she didn't.

She ran all the way around the park with the boys in PE. And was the fastest. The boys were so clumsy. Their big feet didn't seem to go in the same direction. And their arms flapped around. They tripped over their own feet all the time.

She drew a picture of Donald. During history. Her best friend Kate said it didn't look like him. But she thought it did. And then she lost it somewhere and panicked. Lucky that Kate found it again. And lucky it didn't really look like him because everyone would have laughed.

Tips from Jez, Lionel and Friends:

We often see differences and not similarities in others. During your teenage years, you want to fit in. The media show us what is 'in' and what is 'out.'

It takes a strong character to do what YOU want to do. To dress how YOU like. To be comfortable with your body.

Judging people at face value is very shallow and very unhealthy. How often have you found that you have put a label on someone and they turned out to be very different? Thomas Jefferson talked about 'Tyranny of the Majority.'

Get curious to get to know others beyond their looks.

Exercise:

Do you prefer to be a shepherd or a sheep?

Below the surface or your looks, who are you?

Who will you get to know beyond their looks?

"We don't stop at our skin." ~ *Dolores Krieger*
Alternative Therapies in Health and Medicine

Chapter Four

Your Relationship with Food

Tangled up with your relationship with Food?

- You don't like to eat

- You are constantly dieting because you think you are too fat

- You constantly eat too much

QUIZ

Let's see how your relationship with food is.

1. You are eating an evening meal with your family. What do you do?

   a. Eat a similar portion to everyone else and talk about your day. You feel happy to connect with your family and share food and stories.

   b. Eat a larger portion than anyone else. You focus totally on your food and even eat what other people leave on their plate. You do not really connect with other family members and are distracted by their stories as they keep you from your real priority, which is eating.

   c. Eat a smaller portion than anyone else. You focus completely on how every bite will make you fat and try to eat as little as you can without having anyone notice.

2. You are in a sweet shop with some money to spend. What do you do?

   a. You buy a few sweets and enjoy eating them and sharing them with your friends and/or family.

   b. You buy all the sweets you can get for all the money that you have. You leave the sweet shop with bulging pockets and bags. Before you leave the shop, you have already tucked in and all the sweets (probably a few pounds or kilos) have vanished within an hour.

   c. You do not buy any sweets. You never eat sweets. You would never eat sweets. It is well known that sweets make you fat.

3. Your Mum has cooked you a healthy meal which consists of a small portion of chicken, some wholemeal pasta, cooked broccoli and a salad made from raw, green leaves, beetroot, chopped onion and tomatoes. What do you do?

   a. You enjoy and eat all you have on your plate.

   b. You push the vegetables around, ask for a burger and finally resort to covering everything in half a bottle of tomato ketchup. You only eat half of it and have two packets of potato crisps afterwards and a large tub of ice-cream.

   c. You only eat the salad and give the meat and pasta to the dog when no one is watching.

4. You are invited to a friend's house for a meal. Your friend's Mum asks what you like to eat. What do you do?

   a. You reply that you are happy to eat most things.

   b. You reply that you only really like burgers and chips and lots of them, please.

   c. You reply that you don't really like to eat much as you are on a diet.

5. You are looking after a younger child, maybe your brother or sister or maybe a friend's brother or sister. You are sharing your views on eating with him or her. What do you do?

   a. You tell them that it is good to eat a balanced meal so that their body stays strong and grows up healthy.

   b. You tell them that it doesn't really matter what you eat as long as it makes you feel full up.

   c. You tell them that they must not eat much in order to stay skinny.

6. Your body feels out of sorts. You may start a cold or you may be extra tired. What do you do?

   a. You drink an extra glass of water at least three times a day. You eat plenty of fruit and fresh vegetables and get some extra rest.

   b. You eat a large meal with a lot of junk food. You feel better for a while, but after that you feel really ghastly.

    c. You have some fizzy, sugary drinks that make you instantly feel better. You run out of steam after that and feel more tired and sick than before.

7.   You have been to a party and you know you should really take it easy the next day. What do you do?

    a. You rest and do some quiet activities around the home. You increase your intake of water, fruit and vegetables. You feel energised the next day.

    b. You drink coffee or cola and eat chocolate to keep awake. You feel the buzz but you don't feel good.

    c. You ignore how you feel and go to another party that evening.

8.   You go to a restaurant for a celebration with your parents. What do you do?

    a. You order what you like as you enjoy the social occasion and join in with the general festivities.

    b. You order the largest dish and a few side dishes. You eye up your neighbours' plates and eat their leftovers. You go to your stash of chocolate bars after the meal and eat six of them.

    c. You order a side salad and nothing else. You prick your fork into the leaves of lettuce over and over again, so that you take as long over your meal as everyone else does.

9. You have been invited to a Barbecue. What do you do?

   a. Eat a little of everything.

   b. Pile your plate as high as you can with the most fattening foods.

   c. Eat just a dry burger bun without butter.

Mostly A: You have a good understanding of food. You know enough about how food effects you, to keep you healthy and ensure that you grow well. You will likely grow up to stay in tune with what your body needs. Ensure that you allow yourself the odd treat at times too.

Mostly B: Your relationship with food is tangled up! You have a tendency to make food more important than it is. You don't look to food as something that nourishes you and gives you energy. The food you currently eat, reduces your energy. For you it is the 'feel good' factor from mostly empty calories. Educate yourself on nutrition and have a look into what chemical reactions certain foods give. Then adjust your diet to ensure that what you eat actually gives you energy. You may grow up to be overweight and unhealthy if you don't change this habit.

Mostly C: Your relationship with food is tangled up too! You feel that you are fat and that food has made you fat. While that may be the case, it may also be that you are confusing the way your body has changed from child shape to teenage shape with getting fat. You risk giving your body insufficient nutrition. It may be unable to make strong enough bones and organs to sustain you through life and grow up healthy and well. You may want to seek advice as this behaviour can lead to an eating disorder.

Tips from Jez, Lionel and Friends:

This is the age for getting spots. Drinking lots of water can help clear your skin. It also helps to flush out toxins from your system. You will find out what works best for you. If you have eaten a lot of sweets, you notice that you get irritable or tired. Eat salads and raw food at times.

Foods are made to make you buy and eat more. Advertisers want you to buy their products. Even so called healthy foods aren't always healthy. Read the labels.

Exercise:

Write a Food Diary. What food (and drink) passes your lips in 24 hours? Do this for one week.

Eat a new and healthy food each week. Write down what you like.

Chapter Five

Your Relationship with School

Tangled up with your relationship with School?

- You don't like school

- You don't want to learn

- You don't see the point of getting an education when there are many more interesting things going on

Schools go all the way back in history to the ancient Greeks and Romans. In order to govern the vast empires, it was necessary to have a large amount of people being literate and able to use basic chores to fill the large amount of offices. Schools were also started in order to pass on certain knowledge such as religion and language.

In Germany schools were initially invented by the generals in the Prussian army as a way to prepare children (boys) to be ready to enter the army. As you can imagine, the army needs people to listen to commands and to execute orders.

Today the school system is largely based on the model of a teacher standing in front of a classroom of multiple pupils. The pupils are generally seated and only speak when asked. They are quiet and listen or busy doing their work.

Education of young children starts with an exploration of the world. Initially, our parents teach us how they want us to behave and what they want us to know. As we saw, we learn that some behaviour get us praise and other behaviour gets us frowns, scolds or even physical reminders of disapproval.

Our parents sent us to the school of their choice. They may have gone their themselves or like the ethics or it may just be near to where you live. As humans we copy other humans around us. We also seek approval first from our elders and later from our peers. At an early age we start doing what others do.

Your Relationship with Work

Tangled up with your relationship with Work?

- You do not show any sense of responsibility

- You arrive at your job late or not at all

- You don't like the work you do

In the past, people were often obliged to do work that they neither liked nor wanted to do. No one asked them whether they liked or wanted to do the work. They just did it as a means to make money. Things have changed. There is more choice. You may live in a country where work is not the only way to get money. Some cultures have other measures in place to ensure their people get enough money to supply for their needs (social services, guaranteed state income or unemployment insurance).

Recently, there is a lot of talk about the sense of entitlement of younger people. Employers complain that their younger employees feel they should get time off for all kinds of reasons. For a friend's Birthday, for an outing, for a heat wave and for a snow storm. They say that the job is not taken seriously. Employees can get fired when they are absent too often, without a good reason.

Your Relationship with Money

Tangled up with your relationship with money?

- You spend more money than you earn and have

- You have not learned about money management

- You are scared of money

Money is the currency of the world. We don't get taught about money in school and not all of us have the opportunity to learn about money from our parents either. With permission from Ben Tristem*, we have added his easy diagram and explanation to show you the relationship with money.

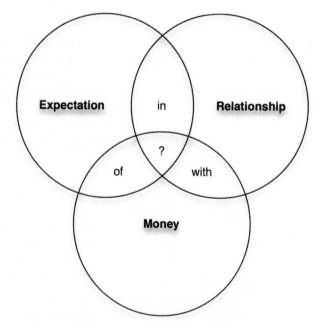

"Expectations affect relationships, usually for the worse. You have a relationship with money, and if you want to

attract it and keep it you'll have to treat it like you would any other life partner. So, what are your expectations in your relationship to money? You get to set the rules of the game, so are you making the game easy to win?"
Ben Tristem, Entrepreneur. www.bentristem.com

Tips from Jez, Lionel and Friends:

School is a preparation for life. It is where you learn and where your social life takes place. Looking back, it is a great opportunity to learn how to relate to others. It is also a good place to prepare you for work.

Make sure that you excel at what you do. If you don't like what you do, move on or change your attitude. If you are in a job that requires higher qualifications to be promoted, be proactive and get those diplomas or degrees.

If you do not like to study, find out what other ways there are to get promoted. Ask if the company has a relationship with other companies that may be a better match with your personality and/or skills. Start your own company.

If you keep doing what you have always done, you will keep getting the same results. Do something different and the result will be different too.

Money is important to teenagers. Make sure you make responsible choices. Some lending institutions make large loans available to young people. Think further than today. You WILL have to pay back loans. They are what they say.... loans. Get really good at tracking where and how you spend your money. Read books such as 'Rich Dad, Poor Dad' by Robert Kyosaki. Create a spreadsheet for your outgoings and make sure you SAVE. However boring it sounds, it is a great habit. The good news is, when you start at this age, you will have a large sum by the time you get to your parents' age!

Exercise:

If you didn't need the money, what kind of work would you do?

Is there a hobby that you can turn into your career (people who's career is also their hobby, live a much happier life)?

How can you market the skills and talents you have to create an income?

Chapter Six

Your Relationship with Peers

Tangled up with your relationship with your Peers?

- You don't relate to people of your own age

- You feel that you are the only one with your particular problems and issues

- You don't have any friends

- You spend your life with your peers only

QUIZ

Let's find out how you relate to your peers.

1. You want to see a movie. What do you do?

   a. You go on your own because you don't dare ask anyone to come with you.

   b. You ask your friends to come with you.

   c. You don't dare ask your friends, so you ask your Mum to go with you.

2. You want to wear your new outfit which does not conform to fashion norms. What do you do?

   a. You don't wear your outfit in front of others, only at home in your bedroom.

   b. You wear your new outfit when you feel like it and ignore the comments you get. After a while other people wear a similar outfit.

c. You never wear your new outfit because you are afraid that others don't like it and will comment on it. You outgrow it and you give it away to your little brother or sister.

3. Your friends all go to a party. You don't want to go as you need to finish some school work. What do you do?

a. You have not been invited. You sit at home alone and read. You can't focus on what you are reading though as you think about the party all the time and the people having a good time without you.

b. You tell them you'll come along another time when you have free time.

c. You go along to please them, but you don't enjoy yourself and are late handing in your work. You get into trouble with your teachers.

4. You don't like to take a relationship further. You want to take time before you get intimate with someone. What do you do?

a. You have not been in a relationship yet although you'd like to be.

b. You tell the person you are with that you want to wait and get to know them better before you take the next step in intimacy. The other person respects you and is happy to wait. If they are not happy to wait, you decide to finish with them.

c. For fear of being rejected you are intimate with everyone. Afterwards, the other person loses interest in you quickly and moves on.

5. You are asked to try a drink or chemical substance. You don't want to. What do you do?

   a. You hide and avoid confrontation with the people who asked you.

   b. You politely decline. If these friends keep asking, you decide to choose new friends with healthier habits.

   c. You say 'yes' to anything they ask, you are afraid to end up without friends.

6. Your friends decide to skip school for the afternoon to go into town. What do you do?

   a. You don't get asked to go along and feel sorry for yourself.

   b. You think about the consequences and decide to join them after school.

   c. Even though you don't want to go, you feel you have to. You get punished at home and at school for playing truant.

7. Someone in your class gets bullied and teased by others. What do you do?

   a. You're the one being bullied.

   b. You tell your friends that it is awful to be bullied, you stand up for the person who is bullied and you don't join in.

   c. You join in because everyone is doing it.

8. A new band is all the rage. Everyone likes the music. You don't. What do you do when everyone goes to the concert?

   a. You don't get asked to go along to the concert and sit at home feeling sad.

   b. You kindly decline when asked to come along to the concert.

   c. You don't even think about it, you just go along to the concert because your friends are going.

9. Your friend wants you to borrow your Mum's car to run her or him home. You know that she will be upset if you take it without asking her. What do you do?

   a. You avoid the question and quickly usher your friend out of the house.

   b. You explain to your friend that your Mum would not like you to take her car. They can either wait until she is available to ask or take a bus home.

   c. You don't hesitate and borrow the car. Your Mum is upset when she finds out.

Mostly A: You have not learned how to relate to your peers. Learn how to communicate with people. Take a course. Read a book. Relax. Learn to accept yourself as you are. Find a hobby that you like where you can have a peer group with whom you can relate.

Mostly B: You are level headed and think ahead. You understand peer group pressure and do not easily give in to other people's demands. You are firmly rooted in your own identity. You have learned how to communicate well. You relate to others in a healthy way.

Mostly C: You are tangled up in your relationships with your peers! You take actions that are not in line with your values and you go against your gut feeling. Make sure to stay safe. You could fall in with the 'wrong crowd' as you constantly give your power away. Learn how to say 'no' and do things on your terms. Trust your own instincts. Remember that you will never find out who YOU are when you constantly do what others suggest and want.

Chapter Seven

Your Intimate Relationships

During teenage years many people have their first intimate relationship. You find that it is nice to be close to someone. You find that you are attracted to boys or girls physically. You discover that being intimate with another person is special.

Boys tend to joke and tease more between one another. When they are with girls, they try the same approach but girls do not always understand or appreciate this. Boys thump each other on the shoulder or slap one another on the back when they are friendly. When they do the same thing to a girl, they hurt her physically, so they must find different ways to express their friendship.

Boys can be very puzzled as to how to approach a girl. They can't thump them on the back and they can't kiss them straight away either. Girls don't all like wolf whistles. In some cultures it is more acceptable to go up to someone and tell them you like them than in others.

Boys and girls have different ways of communicating so their relationships aren't always straight forward. Boys learn that they need to talk to girls in a way that girls like. This can be unfamiliar and make a boy feel quite awkward. Girls tend to be more subtle in their communication. They 'hint' that they like a boy, or they 'drop hints' when they need or want something in a relationship. They get upset when the boy just doesn't get it. Boys wonder why girls don't just ask when they want or need something.

It is useful to know about the differences in communication. It's like visiting a different culture and country. Before your trip there, you read up on the ways of that country, what to do and what not to do and you learn a few phrases in the language of that country. If you intend to spend a lot of time in a particular country, it helps to learn to get by in the language.

It is the same in relationships. If you intend to spend a lot of time with boys, it helps to know what language they speak and how they communicate. If you intend to spend time with girls, you want to get more or less fluent in their language, or at least be able to translate what they say, so that it makes sense to you, in your own language.

Girls want to spend a lot of time together when they like someone. You can see girls hang out together with other girls almost twenty-four-seven. They go shopping together. They talk for hours. They giggle and laugh. They talk more. This makes girls feel connected.

This kind of closeness is claustrophobic to boys. They need space and time to be with their mates, to be physically active, to be competitive and to spend time alone. When boys express their wish to be with their mates, play sports or spend time alone, girls often translate this as the end of their relationship, as in 'girl' language, when you don't want to be with someone all the time, it means you don't like or love them.

It takes time to figure out what the other person means. Don't assume that because a person from another culture has different ways, they are strange. Look at the world through their eyes and from their background and see if you can find a different meaning for the way they communicate? The same is true with boys and girls. When boys get upset, they prefer to work things out on their own. When girls get upset, they prefer to talk about it all the time.

Alan and Barbara Pease write in their excellent book 'Why men don't listen and women can't read maps' that men have an average of 10.000 words per day to get out and women have about 20.000. Here you can see the imbalance. Long after the man/boy has ran out of words, there are still another 10.000 words for a woman/girl to get out that day.

Girls naturally want a lot of attention from their boyfriends. Sometimes they ask for attention in indirect ways. They tell there boyfriends that 'we never spend time together,' or 'you always spend time cleaning your car' which should not be taken literally. It just means 'I like you so much that I would really love to spend more time with you.'

When Jez and Lionel were teenagers, I would find them and a group of their friends bent over a mobile phone, discussing a text message that one of them had just received on their phone from a girl. It said 'do you like me?' The boy wondered if that meant that she liked HIM? There were long discussions about that single message. The boys were divided into two camps. One half thought it did mean that she liked him. The other half was convinced that she didn't. One of their girlfriends was consulted to find out. 'Yes, she likes you, ask if she wants to go out with you' was the reply. 'Are you sure?' They were puzzled.

Boys want to be admired by their girlfriends. Sometimes they show off to get compliments. They compete with their friends to get your attention. Many moons ago, boys and men used to go hunting and brag to one another about their prey. When they like a girl, most boys still show this hunting kind of behaviour.

Boys get close by being intimate. Girls can't get intimate until they feel close to someone. Do you see the catch?

Not only the differences between men and women become apparent but also differences in values, different experiences and a different cultural background play a role in how you get on in a relationship. Teenage years are excellent for getting used to and practice with relationships.

Your Relationship with Boys

Tangled up with your relationship with Boys?

- You don't like boys at all

- The only thing you can think of is boys

- You behave like a boy so they will like you more

Your Relationship with Girls

Tangled up with your relationship with Girls?

- You don't like girls at all

- The only thing you can think of is girls

- You ignore girls because they scare you

A Story:

I just don't understand what she wants, Josh tells me. She is messing me about, one moment she wants this, one moment she wants the complete opposite. I'm out, she can find another boyfriend to control. My mates tell me I'm unavailable, my parents are breathing down my neck as my school work is flagging. My football coach says I'm not engaged and I don't know what to do.

Josh is a lovely young man of seventeen. He has a lot to deal with in his young life. His Mum and Dad are divorced. He and his younger sister live with either parent one week and with the other the next. They have been doing this since Josh was fourteen and keeping track of his possessions at either home is not always easy.

Becky came on the scene three months ago. Lovely and

bubbly. Her laughter is contagious and she has a sharp mind. Josh and Becky sat together during a few history lessons, and the rest is, well, hey, history. They became an item and were seen together more and more.

In the beginning all was great. Josh could do nothing wrong in Becky's pale blue eyes. Her lashes would flutter at his silly jokes, whenever he smiled or even when he looked seriously at her. He felt like a newly discovered hero and thrived under the attention. His confidence went through the roof. He scored goals at football, achieved the highest scores in his exams and enjoyed his chores at home. His sister even said that he was a 'lovely big brother' for about six weeks.

Then everything turned. Becky didn't smile any longer, she did not look at him the way she did used to and everything he did seemed to annoy her and provoke a nasty comment. As far as Josh was concerned, he had not done anything different at all. In short, Josh was puzzled.

How do you know that you are in love? How does it feel?

These are just some of the answers from a variety of young people:

- It feels like you are floating on the a cloud of endless possibilities and dreams.

- It feels like you just got the best prize the world has to offer.

- You think of them.

- You want to be with them.

- You want to know all about them.

- It makes you giddy, and like you just wanna fly.

- It is a beautiful feeling.

- Best feeling ever! Colours brighter, clearer, deeper.

- When I first fell in love, I didn't feel like eating because of all the butterflies in my tummy.

- I don't think I have ever experienced that feeling? Or butterflies in my stomach like people describe? Am I normal?

- Love is going to bed every night longing to be with them. It's when you're asleep you dream about them so even when you're away from them, you can still see them.

Tips from Jez, Lionel and Friends:

Language of boys and girls is different. Don't take the words you hear literally. If you are not sure, ask for an explanation.

Before you commit to a longer relationship, be with a group of friends. There can be a lot of pressure from peers to be intimate. Stay with your own feelings. People respect you more if you do what you want yourself. It builds your character and your identity. Ultimately it feels good to stand your ground and stick to your own principles.

What do you do when you like someone?

You don't know what someone is thinking and whether they like you or not. You can make friends with their friends and become part of their group. The first thing is that you need to talk to them to find out what they are like. Ask questions. People always like to talk about themselves. Display an interest in them. Smile a lot. Be friendly and joke. Don't be too serious. If you don't give it a shot, you'll never know. So, if you meet someone you like, don't be afraid to acknowledge your feelings. Say 'I like you' to the person.

If someone does not respond to your approach, it doesn't automatically mean that they don't like you. Maybe they are shy or insecure. Maybe they consider you 'out of their league' beautiful, intelligent or cool. Do the 'In their shoes exercise' at the end of this chapter.

What to talk about?

You can talk about school, work, interests and hobbies. The more social skills you have, the better. You can practice your social skills by talking to anyone, so when you feel a little nervous when you are attracted to someone you are better at it than someone who hasn't practiced. It is good to realise that other people have interesting lives. Ask how they live, where they live. What they do and like as a family.

Use humour, be light. But don't overuse humour because it gets irritating if you're never serious.

What if you are shy?

Most people are shy to a certain extent. Recognise and acknowledge that you are a bit nervous. Exercise, wear nice clothes, so you feel good about yourself.

What to do when you are not attracted to someone any longer?

It is better to tell someone that you want to finish the relationship than to keep them stringing along. It is always possible that you are not in love any more. It can be upsetting, and that chapter of your life is over. If you think about cheating on the person, it is better to finish before you actually do. It is more honest to you and the other person. You have to think about the long run.

It is never nice to tell someone that you don't want to be with them any more when they are still in love with you. They may feel hurt. You can really feel bad about yourself. It is best to tell them in person and tell them straight away. Give them enough time and respect to get over you. Give them time to heal. Don't give them any hints that you may still be interested when you are not. That is not kind.

Exercise:

Be the first to approach the other after an upset, do not keep score and say 'I was the first one last time' because that is not a relationship, but a competition.

If you are upset, ask yourself what meaning you have linked to the behaviour or communication to be upset, then ask if this could be a misconception and if you have all the information needed to know what the behaviour or communication meant?

In their shoes exercise: Imagine that you are someone of the opposite sex. How would you act, what would you think? How would you react?

What did you learn from the last exercise? And how can you use it to improve your relationships?

Chapter Eight

Your Relationship with Family

Tangled up with your relationship with your siblings and other family?

- You don't like your brothers/sisters

- Your brothers/sisters don't like you

- You don't get on with your grandparents, uncles, aunts etc.

- You feel different and the 'odd' one out in your family

Your Relationship with Society

Tangled up with your relationship with Society and the Law?

- You feel that there are too many rules and regulations in the society where you live

- You challenge the rules and laws with unlawful behaviour

Your Relationship with Nature

Tangled up with your relationship with nature?

- You are not in touch with nature

- You find nature scary or dirty

- You don't like to be outdoors

- You don't know anything about nature

Tips from Jez, Lionel and Friends:

You are part of your family. But you don't choose your family. Can you find something good in every member of your family?

Society has laws to keep us and others safe and make sure that things go orderly. We all have to abide by the laws of our countries. It really makes no difference if you like the laws or not, as you have no power to change them. It is best to stay within the law. Use the energy that you spend on complaining about the law and finding ways to dodge laws more productively. Use your time wisely to do something worthwhile.

We are part of nature. If you haven't been brought up close to nature, it can feel scary or dirty, there are bugs and critters that you may not know. Learn about them, spend time outdoors every day in the fresh air. There is so much more oxygen in nature than indoors!

Chapter Nine

Your Relationship with Your Parents

Tangled up with your relationship with your Parents?

- You feel they don't understand you

- You don't understand your parents

- You don't want to be around your parents

- Your parents have outdated ideas

- Your parents' ideas and your ideas are opposites

- You don't do anything without your parents

QUIZ

How Tangled is your Relationship with your Parents?

1. You and your parents are sitting down to eat a meal at the dining table. What do you do?

    a. You take it in turn to talk about your day and to listen to one another. Your parents, siblings and you each take an interest in each others' day. You discuss any challenges that have come up during the day and any happy events, such as personal achievements and anecdotes.

    b. You eat your meal while you all watch the TV and do not talk. When someone says a word, the others tell them to shut up.

    c. You all quietly sit and check your emails and text messages on your laptop or phone and don't really talk much apart from asking for someone to pass the salt or the butter.

d. You never sit down to eat as a family.

2. You have a problem and want some advice. What do you do?

a. You go to your Mum or Dad and discuss the problem. You either talk about it then and there or agree another suitable time within the next 24 hours.

b. You scream and shout that you need someone's help now! When no one listens you stomp off to your room, slamming all the doors on the way.

c. You sulk and go to your room and hope that either Mum or Dad will notice that you need their help. They might figure it out, but they might not.

d. You don't talk to your parents. You may look on the internet or ask a friend.

3. You are not happy with some of your chosen subjects at school and want to change. What do you do?

a. You talk about it with one or both your parents. You tell them how you feel. They in turn ask you to come up with reasons for your choice and give you advice to consider what consequences the change has for your future. You then make the choice.

b. You shout at your parents that you will quit school. That you hate this particular subject and that you will never go back to the lessons ever again.

c. You bear it quietly and feel that your life is meant to be miserable. During the lessons you switch off and don't really care.

d. You discuss it at school and the subjects are changed without involving your parents.

4. You are concerned about your body. Maybe you have not grown as tall as your peers, maybe you are always tired. Maybe you are worried about new bodily functions such as your sexuality. What do you do?

   a. You approach one of your parents and discuss it with them. Perhaps you talk to both of them.

   b. You are rude to everyone around you for a week, then you forget about it.

   c. You wonder why this is happening to you? Have you done something wrong? You brood about it and talk about it with no one.

   d. You google it or ask a friend at school. You wouldn't dream about speaking about it to your parents.

5. You want to go on a week long trip with friends. You think it is a good idea, but you are not sure if your parents like the idea as this is the first time you go away without an adult.

   a. You discuss it with your parents. You understand their objections and you discuss ways to deal with possible challenges. Your parents, you, your friends and their parents have a Barbecue together before the trip. You agree with your parents on times and frequency to check in with one another.

   b. You tell your parents that you are going away with your friends at an inconvenient time when they are in the middle of something. They don't agree and you end up having a shouting match. You may be grounded for a week and are certainly not allowed to go.

c. You tell no one. What's the point? You know in advance that you are not allowed to go, because nice things simply never happen to you.

d. You tell no one. You book the trip on the internet and send your Mum and Dad an email of the dates. When you leave for your trip there is no one to see you off and when you return, no one seems to notice that you have been gone.

6. You want to go to a party. It ends after the time that you would normally be allowed to stay out. What do you do?

a. You pick a moment that your Mum and Dad are relaxed and in a good mood. You tell them that you would not normally ask them as you know this is past your 'curfew' time, but would like to ask for their permission for this one time to stay out until this particular time. You are indeed back on the agreed time.

b. You stomp into a conversation that Mum and Dad are having and announce that you are going to stay out most of the night and if they don't agree, you will leave home forever. You don't listen to any of their concerns. You shout 'I will do what I want anyway' and leave the room.

c. You don't even bother to ask. Nice things don't ever happen to you (remember?). If you can be bothered, you might sneak out of your window to join the party. But that is very unlikely.

d. You just go, no one will notice, they didn't last week, or the week before, or the week etc.

7. You strongly disagree with your Mum or Dad. What do you do?

    a. You talk about it during dinner or another suitable moment when you have their full attention. You tell them why you don't agree with them and you tell them your point of view. At the end of the discussion you all agree to disagree and leave the discussion in peace.

    b. You all shout and scream. There are a lot of 'you always's' 'you never's' and the conversation doesn't lead anywhere. No one is really listening to each other. At the end, you are all angry.

    c. You don't say anything, but they may figure out why you are sulking (again). No one will listen to you anyway, so why bother?

    d. You just go your own way. Everyone in your family does. It keeps the peace.

8. Your friend has lied to you. You are really upset. What do you do?

    a. You discuss this with your Mum or Dad. You tell them how upset you are and why. You firmly believe that lying is wrong. Your friend firmly believes that you can't hurt a friend, even if it means you have to lie. This has led to your upset. All upsets are created by having different rules and believes. You remember that your friend is probably as upset as you are and make the first move to make amends.

    b. You shout, scream and cry. You cut your friend off and do not want to have anything to do with her/him ever again. Your parents say 'see, I told you so, she/he is a 'no good friend'.

    c. You hide in your room and stay under the covers. You feel paralysed. How could he/she? You take the meaning of your friend lying to mean that you are not worth the truth. You feel miserable for a week and finally emerge with great, big bags under your eyes. Your parents try to coax you out of this mood, but are not successful and finally give up.

    d. You say 'next' and don't bat an eyelid and hang out with other friends. You tell no one.

9.   Your boyfriend/girlfriend wants to move on to the next stage of intimacy. You don't want to, but feel awkward about telling them. What do you do?

    a. You talk about it with your Mum or Dad, you ask for their advice. You take their opinions and advice into consideration and tell your boyfriend/girlfriend that you are not ready for this yet.

    b. You get angry with your little brother and you are irritated with your Mum's new hairstyle. Your Dad also gets a sneer when he tries to kiss you goodbye for school. Your parents in turn get upset with you and you end up with an argument.

    c. You are withdrawn and stop eating for a few days. Your parents want to talk, but you clam up.

    d. I tell my boyfriend/girlfriend no.

Mostly A: You have a good relationship with your parents. You all communicate well and you ask your parents for advice when needed. Make sure that you also build relationships with friends and other adults, so that you have a balanced support group with plenty of choice.

Mostly B: Your relationship with your parents is tangled up! None of you communicate well. You are all reactive and do not listen to one another. Of course at times, you will be emotional, but if this is you behave like this all the time, I suggest learn how to communicate more effectively and if you can, persuade your parents to come along to the course.

Mostly C: Your relationship with your parents is also tangled up! You have learned to behave like a victim. This does not get you anywhere. Of course you will feel that you don't have control over situations some of the time, but if this is consistent and all the time, get some help and learn how to take charge of your life.

Mostly D: Your relationship with your parents is non-existent! Maybe you are very independent. Maybe you have parents that do not relate to you or you to them. Maybe there is space to create a relationship with your parents if you and them wish to do so. You may feel very alone and lonely. Make sure to have relationships in your life that you can trust and build on.

A Story:

Dear Diary, I am devastated. No one understands me. Mum and Dad are splitting up. And they told me last year that whatever would happen and whoever would separate, THEY never would. They NEVER would!!! Well, maybe I should have known. Mum and Dad never really DO anything together. But they seemed to really like it that way. It never bothered me.

It really only dawned on me last week at my best friend Sophie's house. When Sophie's mum put a large dish of freshly baked vegetables on the table. Drizzled with olive oil, some crushed rosemary and coarse sea salt. Everyone was cheerful and talking about their day. We never even eat together. Let alone talk about anything. Even remembering, my mouth waters. I did decline the chicken as my own whole family is veggie, but I almost had second thoughts when I saw Sophie and her family tucking in. I sometimes really envy Sophie.

And now my life is over. My sisters seemed fine with it. Took it all in their stride. It was so strange, the way Mum and Dad told us only three weeks ago. I knew there was something weird going on. Picture this, Mum and Dad on the sofa. A polite space between them. They never talk to us together. And they never sit on that sofa together. It is mostly used for books and coats.

Mum and us will stay in the house. Dad will move out as soon as he's found something suitable. So many questions. I feel so alone and so confused.

My sister Lana was sulking and so angry. She stormed out of the room. Lana never talks. Angeline tries to win Dad over. She is sweet as pie. As if her being nice can make it better. As if she is at fault for Mum and Dad splitting up and by being nice, she can make it all undone.

Then on Monday there was a panic. Lana was missing. She just took off and sent everyone a message on Facebook from Maggie's house who lives in the next town. Picture that, she had taken her Birthday money from Granddad, bought a train ticket and just took off without saying goodbye or anything. Mum and Dad were livid. And then there were no more posts for two days when she was with uncle Eric who lives two hundred miles away!

Dad sleeps on the sofa now. Yes, the very sofa they sat on when they told us. He does not seem to have hairbrush or his shaving things so he looks very old now, with his grey stubble and uncombed hair. Or maybe it is a new look. Really doesn't suit him. Anyway, the third post was from cousin Ralf's, who moved to his wife's village three years ago. Mum phoned Ralf and his wife and they are having a chat with Lana. I think her anger has gone now.

The travel probably took it out of her. But I'm still upset. No one takes notice of me. I suppose it is because I'm just stuck in the middle. Not angry and sulky like Lana. Not sweet as pie like little Angeline. Just being me. Smiling, lovely Tanni. No one knows what goes on inside me. Not even Sophie.

By the way, I really do like Callum. He is Sophie's big brother. But he is not interested in anything but his football. And certainly not in me, his little sister's friend. He lives for his football. Picture this, lanky eighteen year old guy. Football shorts and football boots. Comes into the kitchen door all sweaty. Leaves muddy foot prints on the kitchen floor. Me and Sophie making cake. I giggle and can't stop laughing.

Poor Callum. I think he thought I was laughing at HIM. I eat cake. I eat more cake. I eat so much cake that it makes me feel sick. And then I started my period and my tummy was so very sore. Went to bed early in my yummy snugly pyjamas. The pink ones. But I really like Callum. Shall I tell Mum? No, she's way too busy. I'll talk to Sophie's Mum. Tomorrow. Sleep now.

You may think that adults have all the answers, well that is not the case. As teenagers, they may not have had great role models for relationships. When you're an adult yourself you will find that life still throws challenges at you. That will never stop. You learn how to deal with situations and emotions and how to deal with life's upsets and pains. You learn that no one can make you feel bad. The only person who can make you feel bad, is you. And the only person who can make you feel happy, is you.

You learn that there isn't a situation outside yourself that can cause you to feel bad either. It is what you choose to feel about that situation that makes you feel either unhappy or happy.

There are many things that we learn from our parents. We get rewarded for being 'a good girl' or 'a good boy' by our parents. This encourages us to continue this behaviour into adulthood. We have an in built system that tells us that we have been 'good' or that we have been 'bad'.

'There is nothing either good or bad but thinking makes it so'   Shakespeare (Hamlet)

During teenage years, it is not uncommon to rebel against your parents. In other words, you explore being 'bad' and push the boundaries. You do not necessarily want to adopt the same views as your parents. You question whether your parents' values are the ones you want to adhere to, or not.

Between the ages of fourteen and nineteen, your friends and peers generally become more important to you than your parents. You spend more and more time away from your parents and your home family and spend more and more time with friends, at school and at clubs.

Many parents find this a very challenging time. They see their little boy or girl mature in front of their eyes. Of course all parents know that this will happen at some stage, yet most parents are not prepared when it finally hits them that little Johnny or Jenny is growing up.

What parents struggle with most:

Your behaviour has changed.

From the conforming boy and girl, you now have an opinion, you talk less with them, you discuss your plans with your friends and not with them. This makes parents feel really out of control and see monsters around every corner and danger behind every bush. Believe it or not, this is because they love you and want to protect you against all that is lurking in the big world. As I said before, most parents have their own challenges (financial problems, problems at work, problems in their relationship, problems with their own parents and many more) and when you grow up and start to announce that you want to do 'grown up stuff', they FREAK OUT!

Your looks have changed.

You grew steadily after you were born. Parents celebrate the milestones, you smiled, walked, talked, spoke, wrote, ran, cycled, lost your milk teeth and scored your first goal in football. All great reasons for celebration. When you come to teenage hood, the first thing that parents do, is forget that they were EVER teenagers themselves. Or they remember too well the problems they landed themselves in and want to protect you from falling in the same traps.

You hang out with your friends and not with them.

Before you were a teenager you spent time at school, time at home and time with friends. Around 60% of your time was spent at home, around 30% at school and around 10% with friends. This changes to around 50% or less at home, 30% at school and 20% with friends. During holidays it becomes around 50% or more with friends or at clubs. And the home time includes your sleeping time, so most parents do not really consider this as 'home time'.

You share less of how you are doing with them and more with your friends.

They know less about you. Before, they knew everything about you. They knew where every scrape on your body came from, what every nuance in your voice meant and what you liked to eat and how much before you were a teenager. They need to adjust to their new role, which is less nurturing and more supporting. And they need to adjust to your changes. Particularly irritating to teenagers is the parent who second guesses you constantly and still treats you as a child, 'I made your favourite dish' 'I invited Danny because you have been friends with him since you were six', 'I arranged a visit to Grandma's house for you in the holidays, you loved it when you were ten'.

Your hormones get in the way.

You snap. You growl. You withdraw. You have roller coaster moods. One moment you are happy. The next moment you are desperately unhappy. You, the one of even moods and sunny nature! Exclaims your Mum. Yes, me, I am depressed. I have a spot on my nose! I was going to wear the new top that you bought me, but that doesn't go with the spotty face so I much rather disappear into the wall than look like THIS!

You see short term.

What is important is now. What is important is ME. And what is important is that I have IT NOW. Regardless of what IT is. This is the age of selfishness. You are oblivious to other peoples needs, your little brother or sister doesn't exist (or no more than the furniture) and your chores in the house, who cares?

You look more mature than you are.

In your eyes you may not look like an adult. In the eyes of your parents you are tall, fully grown and they see that the world judges you as an adult. When you still behave like a child, the world judges you harshly, which you may not understand. Here is an example from when Jez was fifteen. He and a friend thought it would be fun to measure their strength by pushing over a shed. So they set to work and yes, they pushed the shed over. They felt very powerful and strong. Yeah! Some people watched their endeavours from an upstairs window and phoned the police to say that some vandals had just pushed their neighbours shed over. The police arrived and took Jez and his friend to spend a night in a cell. A bit of fun ended because they chose to use their strength in a silly way. They learned from that experience.

You have so many things on the go and your school work is suffering.

Society has designed it so that we need to spend our teenage years in school, making big decisions. We have great brain capacity to learn at this stage, but there is so much else going on. A scientist has suggested that it would be great to give teenagers either five years off to grow up and come to terms with their bodily and emotional changes. From fourteen to nineteen you work through all the stuff you need to work through, then from nineteen to twenty two you do your schooling and from twenty two to twenty six you do your professional training, university or vocational. What happens now is that your hormones play havoc and you have a budding and thriving social life. School is really not the first thing on your mind. You need to juggle all these very important commitments and have learned to schedule them all in. Worst case scenario is that you haven't learned and keep making mistakes.

Tips from Jez, Lionel and friends:

Your parents want the best for you. Remember that they are probably just as anxious about what is happening to you as you are yourself. Ask them for their advice. Tell them if you are insecure about something.

If you do not feel that you can confide in your parents, seek another adult that can help you. It really helps to have someone else 'on your team.'

Your parents also want to see you happy. They don't always understand that you need to learn the different emotions in life. Life does have sad moments, you will be upset, scared, irritated and angry. Tell your parents that you will get over it. They may be concerned that you don't communicate. Give them a sign that you still love them.

Exercise:

Imagine that you are a Mum or a Dad. You have a child, he or she is your age. He or she is behaving like you do. How would YOU feel in their shoes?

What can you do to keep the relationship with your parents going?

Write down 100 things that are great about your parents (what that does is change your focus from what is wrong about them to what is positive about them).

Chapter Ten

A Chapter for Parents

Congratulations! You have become the proud (?) parent of a teenager!

Parenting teenagers can be such fun and such heartache.

Here are some suggestions to make your life easier, keep your sanity and your relationship with your son or daughter intact.

What happened to my nice little boy/girl?

Teenage years are the years that our sociable children become selfish teenagers (overnight). Their manners are lost to the world. We teach them to share (nicely) and they keep everything to themselves. We teach them to say 'please' and they grunt. We teach them to say 'thank you' and they grunt.

They become self absorbed, they sleep half the morning (or the whole morning), their dress sense is as far opposite of ours as possible and their habits seem to have changed to nothing but offend those they previously pleased.

We accept our children as children and as parents, we need to make a shift when they become teenagers. Our attitude and our approach need to change.

Our little Johnny becomes John, fast on his way to be a man, just like other men around us.

Our precious Mandy becomes Amanda and her teenage years are filled with experimenting at being a woman.

The British TV comedian Harry Enfield had a marvellous character by the name of Kevin. Kevin was a well behaved, amicable twelve year old, with clean clothes, polite manners (he said his 'pleases and thank you's'), who did everything to fit in with his parents and family.

Overnight, when Kevin turned thirteen, he transformed completely. His hair was uncombed and unwashed, he wore a baseball cap back to front with a lock of hair in front of his eyes. He would not look anyone in the eyes and his face was covered in spots. He would grunt versus communicate in words and he wore low slung jeans that dragged on the floor.

Kevin is the stereotypical teenager. The parents' nightmare of what happens in teenage-hood. The teenage years are generally the most challenging years for parents. Loosing control over your child's life can be scary.

When parents are scared, the first reaction tends to be to want to regain control. Childhood measures of discipline are often tried and often fail. More drastic measures are then used, which tend to fail again. They not only fail, they have the opposite to the desired effect.

Very often these measures alienate our children and destroy the trust and respect, which are the basis of any relationship. In order to receive trust and respect from another, we first of all need to give trust and respect first.

How can you stay friends with your teenage child and keep them safe at the same time?

The child does not understand that the parent fears for their wellbeing. In their eyes, the parents spoil their fun.

Building relationship needs to start long before your child becomes a teenager. Encouraging and supporting their strengths and talents must be a red thread throughout their childhood. This doesn't change during the teenage years.

Authentic versus authoritative parenting is called for. Tell them your true feelings. Tell them that you are concerned for their wellbeing. Consider their feelings too. Discussing topics and areas of friction and coming to a mutually acceptable solution is the way forward.

As parents we often want to make things better for our children. We want them to be happy. We don't want them to be sad, frustrated or angry. However, these emotions belong with experiencing life as much as being happy, excited and proud do. It is much more powerful to teach your teenager that these are feelings that they will have at times than to make things better for them.

Offering choices rather than telling is important.

Use positive language to your teenager. 'You can't go out tonight' will give a negative reaction. 'You can go out two nights this week, which nights would you like to choose?' gives your teenager a sense that he/she is in control, is being treated with respect and given choice.

Treating your teenager as a child most certainly creates friction.

I am reminded of the Mum whom I worked with a few years ago. She was desperately sad that her son of seventeen was not the same any more as when he was ten and twelve, even fourteen. When he was younger, she had a great relationship with him. He opened up to her. They talked. For hours. Now he was closed. Awkward. Did not talk to her. And if he did, it was in monosyllables. In passing. She was scared. Did not know what had happened to her lovely boy?

Boys grow up to be men. Men on the whole have less need to talk about things that they occupy their minds. They more likely mull things over in their mind and come up with a solution. Read: Men are from Mars, Women are from Venus by John Gray. Men go into their caves when stressed, women talk to their friends when stressed. Of course we all have masculine and feminine energies, so this is not set in stone. You may want to find situations for your son to open up. My eldest used to talk when I was in the car with him and his younger brother during walks. Make sure that you do give your children the opportunity to talk when needed. During teenage years, they may prefer to talk with you in private, rather than at the dinner table with the whole family present.

Your spouse or another adult may become more important during these years.

It is not always easy to find that the person your teenager confides in is not you any longer! Often they need another perspective. They may want to talk about issues they have with you. Allow and even encourage your teenager to do this. It is a healthy part of growing up. Mostly, adults do not only have one sounding board either, we have different resources that allow us to communicate the different aspects of our personalities. Boys may gravitate towards their father. The way the male body and psyche works is easier modelled and understood from another male's perspective.

Be flexible and expect change.

A Single Mum. Two children. Her daughter away at university. And a son. Twelve. On Saturday evenings Mum supplied nibbles and fizzy drinks and she and her son would curl up on the sofa to watch X-factor. Same son. Fifteen. Did not want to spend all his Saturday nights watching X-factor with Mum. Mum panicked. Did he get in with the wrong crowd? He spoke less. The odd word. She had no longer a detailed report on his whereabouts and his thoughts and feelings.

A Dad. No boy is to come near his little girl! Not in his lifetime. She is precious and he needs to protect her. His daughter Jenny is thirteen and tall. She has developed breasts, her hair is lovely, silky and long. She uses make up during weekends. She has many girl friends. They hang out together. One morning Jenny goes to school in a skirt just above the knee. Comes home in a skirt just below her bum. Dad explodes. Shouts. Jenny runs to her room. Sulks. Stupid old man. Old fashioned tyrant.

Jenny needs to talk. She is rapidly becoming a woman. That is the way women deal with stress. Dad is not in favour in discussing the family problems with anyone. Dad deals with his own stress by being silent and on his own. The way men do.

Expect that your teenager can solve problems that are in proportion to his age and ability.

Another Mum. Son is thirteen. He gets teased at school. Should she get involved? Talk to the other parents? She loves her son. What can she do? Talk to him endlessly? Stand up for him? Mum is at her wits ends. During her session she decides that she will tell him that she trusts him. To do the right thing. That he is strong. And a great kid. And loved. And that he has the innate wisdom how to deal with life's challenges.

"Freedom is not worth having if it does not include the freedom to make mistakes."
Mahatma Gandhi

She goes away. And does what she sets out to do. Everything in her being wants to protect her son. But part of her wisdom knows that what is best is to let him deal with his challenges and learn. The first time he will not do this perfectly. He may mess up. That is the way we learn. By making mistakes. We make a mistake the first time, then we learn. The next time we do a better job. The more we get to practice ANYTHING, the better we get at it.

Ask your teenager what they need and want and how you can support them.

Cindy is fourteen. She is visiting an aunt in a foreign country. Cindy has grown up in the countryside of her own country. She loves being in a town and is curious to discover the shops and variety of new experiences. For the first time in her life, Cindy is away from her parents and her own culture. Cindy has arrived at her relatives' home with only very short tops and shorts. The town is conservative and her aunt knows that Cindy's clothing may be perceived as provocative. Her aunt asks about the dress code in Cindy's home country and goes on to explain that the town has a different dress code. She asks if she can give her some direction and advice. Cindy agrees. They buy some cardigans to cover the bare flesh when out of the home. Cindy understands and is happy to wear the cardigans.

Use humour!

- You will embarrass your teenager, no matter what you do. Have you ever met a parent who never embarrassed their teenager? Turn it around. Your job is to embarrass your teenager. It is in your job description. Laugh about it together.

- Joke with your teenager. Take him or her serious but make fun with them, not about them. Show that you are interested in what they are interested. Do not dismiss their passions and obsessions.

Let them know that you still love them!

- At times they still need a cuddle, make sure to notice and make time for them.

- So much is changing during these years, your love

for them may be the only unchanging force and haven to return to.

- Find out when they want you to tell them that you love them.

- Make time to have time with your teenager. They need much more time on their own and to be with their peers. Make agreements about how much time they spend with their peers during the week for younger teenagers and how much time you'd like to spend with them.

What NOT to do:

- Kiss them in front of their friends

- Tell their boyfriend/girlfriend that they still sleep with their teddy bear

- Kiss them at the school gate

- Ruffle their hair in public

- Use their pet name in public

- Show their baby pictures to their boy/girl friend

- Treat them like a child

- Ignore them

A great comedy to watch is 'The Water Boy' where Adam Sandler plays Bobby Boucher with the mother that never adjusted to her son growing up. Although a comedy, there is a lot of truth of what parents should not do to their teenagers.

During teenage years, you may find that you want to let go of your parenting and focus on other projects. There can be times that your teenager needs you and really wants you to be there for them.

The following sentence from 'A Course of Miracles' has helped a lot of people during the years of parenting teenagers:

'All communication is either a cry for help or an expression of love, responding to a cry for help with another cry for help, guarantees escalation. The correct response to a cry for help is an expression of love'. Could this be what is meant by 'turn the other cheek?' It is very tempting to respond to anger with anger, to a sneer with another sneer. Yet, staying calm and say something like: 'I hear you are really upset, just to let you know that I am here for you if you need me' can diffuse a situation.

Also look into The Centre for Non Violent Communication

A useful question to ask when your teenager has said or done something that you are upset about is 'What else could it mean?' We often just take one meaning for a behaviour. Asking the above question at least opens up options that there are different explanations possible that you may not have considered.

At times it may seem that your teenager has deliberately cut all communication channels. You are not getting through. They have checked out. Doing the same thing over and over again doesn't work. You may want to choose to talk to your child's soul instead. I know it sounds whacky, but working with the energetic versus the physical field can help shift and transform a relationship.

What you can do is meditate, either sitting or walking in nature and just connect to your own heart and soul and then to your child's heart and soul. From your soul to his or her soul, you speak what is on your heart. Not blaming. Not angry. Loving. Try it and see. It is a way that many of my clients have worked with situations where talking was not an option.

Another 'out there' idea is working with the Ho'pono-pono. An ancient Hawaiian mantra that you can use and say for any situation and relationship. Read 'Zero Limits' by Joe Vitale if you want to learn the background.

For now it may just be enough to say silently or aloud:

'I'm sorry

Please forgive me

I love you

Thank you'

Practice forgiveness, this is one of the most powerful tools to help stuck moments move forward. Ultimately, when we do not forgive, we stay in the stuck energy ourselves and our own life becomes stagnant. Forgiving does not mean condoning or forgetting. Forgive yourself first. Is there anyone else you need to forgive?

Tips from Jez, Lionel and Friends:

There are many questions that we still want to ask our parents. We still want to talk with them. We often felt that they do not want to spend time with us. They are embarrassed about who we have become.

However scary, stay connected to your teenager and realise that ultimately, this is just a phase in your and their lives. Like a winter season which can be cold, but you can also dress warmly and wait for spring.

Teenagers will come through this time. They need the stability of a secure home at all times. They need to know that they are still welcome in your home. They need to know that deep down you love them and always will.

Exercise:

Write down 100 things that are great about your teenage son/daughter (what that does is change your focus from what is wrong about them to what is positive about them).

Other Useful Books:

Biddulphs, Steve - *Raising Boys* Harper Thorsons

Brizendine, Louann MD - *The female Brain* Bantam

Canfield, Jack and Mark Victor Hansen - *Chicken Soup for the Teenage Soul:Stories of Life, Love and Learning* Vermillion

Covey, Sean - *The 7 Habits of Highly Effective Teens: The Ultimate Teenage Success Guide* Simon & Schuster Ltd.

DiRuscio Cooper, Alexandra - *So, What?!: A Teen's Guide to What Really Matters* Create Space

Faber, Adele - *How to Talk So Kids Will Listen and Listen So Kids Will Talk* Picadilly Press Ltd.

Freeman, Cynthia and Cliff Wilson - *Money Does Grow on Trees* Magic Penny Pub

Hines, Gill and Alison Baverstock - *Whatever!: A Down-to-Earth Guide to Parenting Teenagers* Piatkus Books

MacCoby, Eleanor - *The Two Sexes-Growing up apart, coming together* Harvard University Press

Madanes,Cloe - *Relationship Breakthrough: Create outstanding relationships in every area of your life* Rodale

McGraw, Jay - *Life Strategies for Teens* Simon & Schuster Ltd.

Kiyosaki, Robert and Sharon L. Lechter- *Rich Dad Poor Dad for Teens: Money - What You Don't Learn in School* Little, Brown & Company

Mitchell, Susie - *Sat Nav for the Soul* My Voice Publishing

Pease, Allan and Barbara - *Why men don't listen and women can't read maps* Orion

Robbins, Anthony - *Notes from a Friend: A Quick and Simple Guide to taking Charge of Your Life* Pocket Books

Rosenberg, Marshall Ph D. - *Non-Violent Communication: A Language of Life* Puddle Dancer Press

Schottky-Osterholt, Connie Dr. - *Finding Your Forever Love: Creating and Keeping the Magic in Your Relationship* Morgan James Publishing

Slocum, Loren - *Life Tune Ups Your Personal Plan to Find Balance, Discover Your Passion, and Step Into Greatness* Globe Pequot Press

Smith, Marlon - *What's Up* Inst of Karmic Guidance www. successbychoice.com

Stoneman, Jacqui - *What am I? What do I Want to do?* My Voice Publishing

Spezzano, Chuck - *How to Save the World: Friends Helping Friends* My Voice Publishing

Spezzano, Chuck - *If it Hurts it isn't Love: Secrets of Successful Relationships* I Mobius

Other Resources:

Facebook Group - Parenting Teenagers

Facebook Group - Teenage Relationships - Untangling Your Heart Strings

One World Academy   www.owayouth.com

Youth Coaching Academy www.youthcoachingacademy. com

Jos Slocum   www.josslocum.com

Event for Teenagers:

Global Youth Leadership Summit - The Anthony Robbins Foundation, www.anthonyrobbinsfoundation.org

Lightning Source UK Ltd.
Milton Keynes UK
UKOW050857250212

187904UK00001B/47/P